T0193450

Hunter's Hero
My Mommy has Breast Cancer

Archway Publishing books may be ordered through booksellers or by contacting:

Archway Publishing
1663 Liberty Drive
Bloomington, IN 47403
www.archwaypublishing.com
844-669-3957

ISBN: 978-1-6657-3101-0 (sc)
ISBN: 978-1-6657-3100-3 (e)

Print information available on the last page.

Archway Publishing rev. date: 11/02/2022

Hunter's Hero
My Mommy has Breast Cancer

Written by Shannon Pierce
Illustrated by Katie Yost

For my son Hunter and all the mommies and
children that hear the words "breast cancer".
You are strong. You are brave.
You are not alone.

My hero is my Mommy.
She has a scar like me.

But, her scar is from
breast cancer
she found at age thirty.

She felt a
lump
and went
to the doctor
straight away.

It moved,
felt small,
round in shape...
all good signs,
so they say.

First, a **mammogram** flattened her boobies like a pancake.

Then, an **ultrasound**. A **biopsy**. Then, we wait...

...and wait some more.
Every phone call sends a jolt of nerves
shaking her to the core.

Until...

...the call we've been waiting for.

"You have breast cancer," the doctor said.

Stage 0

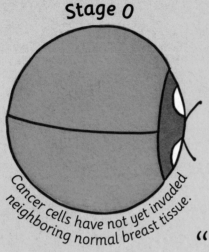

Cancer cells have not yet invaded neighboring normal breast tissue.

Stage 1

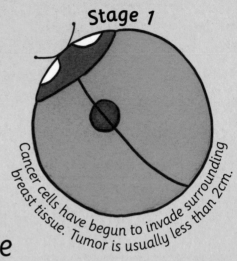

Cancer cells have begun to invade surrounding breast tissue. Tumor is usually less than 2cm.

"It is stage one, but we should address it urgently."

Stage 4

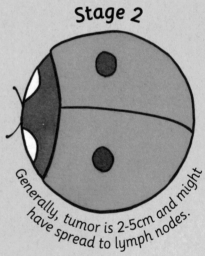

Metastatic, cancer cells have spread to other parts of the body.

Stage 2

Generally, tumor is 2-5cm and might have spread to lymph nodes.

Stage 3

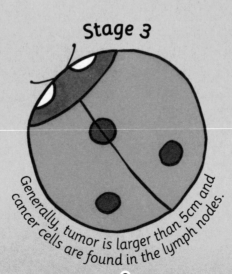

Generally, tumor is larger than 5cm and cancer cells are found in the lymph nodes.

Trying not to panic,
Mommy took notes nervously.

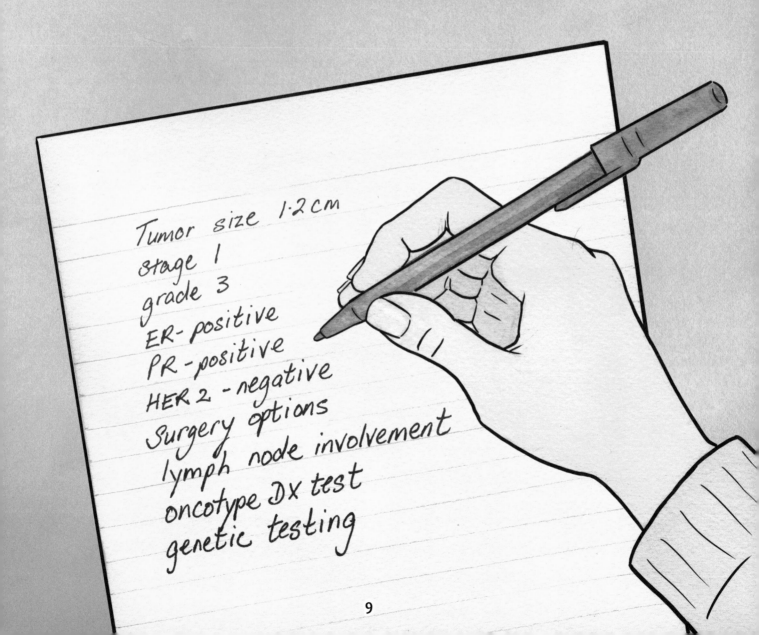

Tumor size 1.2 cm
stage 1
grade 3
ER-positive
PR-positive
HER 2 - negative
Surgery options
lymph node involvement
oncotype Dx test
genetic testing

It's okay to feel scared,
it's okay to feel sad.

Especially when what
happens to mommy is bad.

Breast cancer – a life hurdle
nobody wants to face.

But it's in moments of strength
unknown that we find grace.

The **oncologist** explained
what the treatment plan would be:

Surgery...

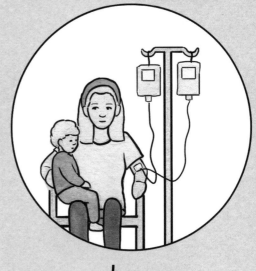

chemo...

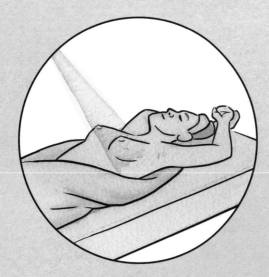

radiation...

and hormone therapy.

It's all so much to consider, so much to take in. All of a sudden our whole world was in a tailspin.

13

Plus if I'm going to have
a brother or sister,

Mommy and Daddy have **IVF** to consider.

My Mommy chose breast conservation - **lumpectomy**.

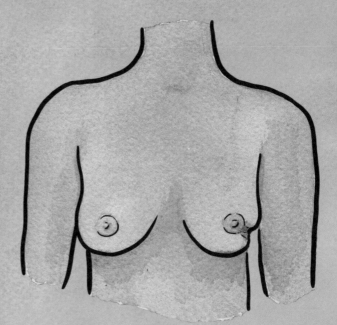

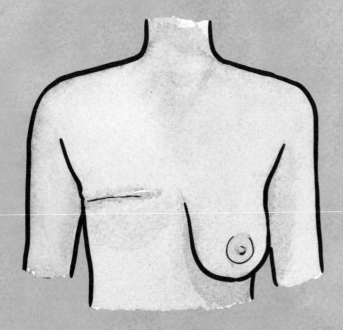

Some mommies lose one... or both boobies - **mastectomy**.

Some mommies have their **breasts reconstructed** (one or two).

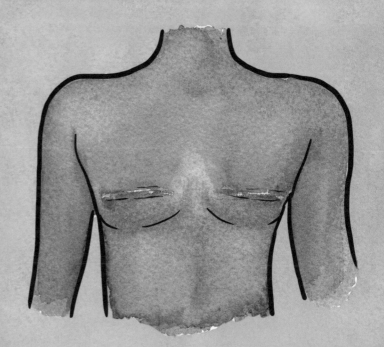

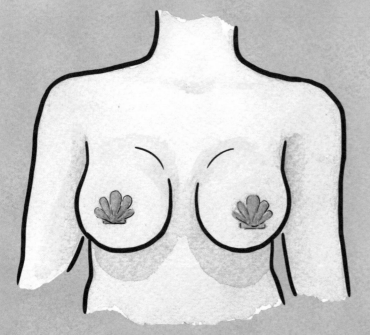

With some kind of nipple or other *fancy tattoo!*

My mommy says boobies
don't define who women are.

Here on earth or in the sky,
every mommy is a star.

Chemo can make
your hair fall out,

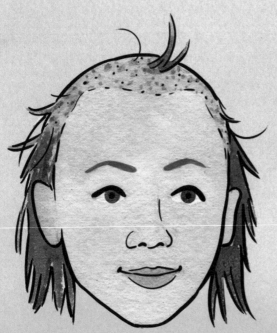

a cold cap
might help.

Some mommies lose
no hair... some hair...

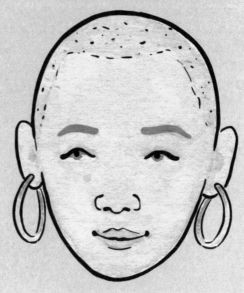

or rock their
bald scalp.

Chemo can also cause
early **menopause.**

"Hot flashes... night sweats...
ugh! I feel like such a Grandma!"

Chemo comes in rounds,
radiation is every day,

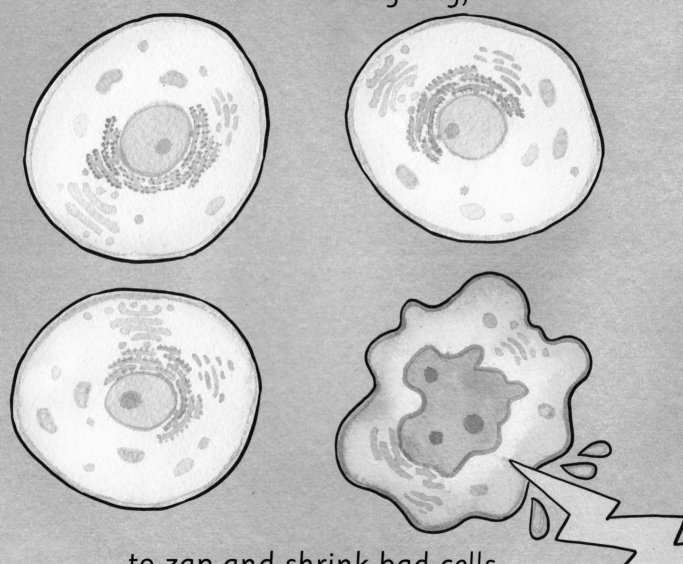

to zap and shrink bad cells
with high-energy rays.

When treatment is over,
there is more healing to do.

Be kind to mommy
    on sunny days
and when she is blue.

It's different for young women
with breast cancer—for sure.
THANK YOU for reading my story
to help find a cure.

All mommies are heroes
with boobies of all sizes and shapes.
Mine just happens
to wear a **pink cape**!

Printed in the United States
by Baker & Taylor Publisher Services